Makoto Tateno
Steal Moon
vol 2
スティール ムーン
June

Translation	Sachiko Sato
Lettering	Replibooks
Graphic Design	Michelle Mauk
Editing	Stephanie Donnelly
Editor in Chief	Fred Lui
Publisher	Hikaru Sasahara

English Edition Published by
DIGITAL MANGA PUBLISHING
A division of DIGITAL MANGA, Inc.
1487 W 178th Street, Suite 300
Gardena, CA 90248

www.dmpbooks.com

First Edition: August 2009
ISBN-10: 1-56970-101-6
ISBN-13: 978-1-56970-101-0

1 3 5 7 9 10 8 6 4 2

Printed in Canada

Steal Moon
スティール ムーン
2
立野真琴
MAKOTO TATENO
presents

StealMoon
スティール ムーン

THE CITY IS UNDER SURVEILLANCE...
...DAMMIT –
IT'S NO GOOD.
I CAN'T SLEEP!
...BY THE MOON.
WHAT THE HELL'S HAPPENED TO THIS TOWN...?
AND NOW, THIS CITY NAMED "AKATSUKI" IS NOW KNOWN AS...

..."THE CITY WITHOUT SLEEP."

SteelMoon
スティール ムーン
♯5

IS "OSIRIS" DEAD?
NO.
WE FAILED AGAIN.

IT'S SURE GIVING US A HARD TIME. IT'S BEEN A MONTH ALREADY.
NO - THREE WEEKS.
THERE'S STILL ONE MORE WEEK 'TIL THE NEXT FULL MOON. WE'VE GOT TO DO SOMETHING BY THEN.

YEAH, YOU'RE RIGHT.

HMM...
IT'S GOING TO BE AWFULLY CLOSE.

IT'S BEEN THREE WEEKS -
SINCE "HE" DISAPPEARED.
KCHAK
I'M BACK -

WELCOME HOME, NOZOMI!
THANKS...
BUT YOU GUYS -
ぐちゃ
CLUTTER
TRY NOT TO MAKE SUCH A MESS, WILL YOU?
SIGH -
BUT THERE ARE SO MANY COOL THINGS IN YOUR ROOM, NOZOMI!
WOW -
THIS IS NOT FOR KIDS!
ばっ
WHISH!
BAD!
MEANIE!
WAIT ANOTHER FIVE YEARS OR SO.
NOZOMI...
HM?
WHERE DID YOU FIND THIS, ANYWAY?

YOU...
LIKE GIRLS?
WHY...
ARE YOU IN LOVE WITH COYOTE?
TWINGE
UH...OF COURSE! THAT GOES WITHOUT SAYING...
THEN WHY?
NOZOMI -
I LOVE YOU, NOZOMI.
YOU MAY NOT BELIEVE ME, BUT...
I LOVE YOU.
...WHAT ARE YOU TALKING ABOUT?

...I'M *NOT* IN LOVE WITH HIM.
THAT TRAITOR -
HE TRICKED US... USED US...
AND SCREWED UP THIS ENTIRE CITY!
SINCE THAT DAY,
THIS CITY HAS KNOWN NO SLEEP.
CONSTANTLY UNDER THE PRESSURE OF THE "MOON'S" GAZE,
THE RESIDENTS HAVE FALLEN PREY TO INSOMNIA, AND SOME EVEN TO NEUROSIS.
THOSE WHO COULD NO LONGER STAND IT ABANDONED THEIR HOUSES IN THE CITY.
AND YET, NO ONE EVEN KNOWS THE REASON BEHIND THIS SURVEILLANCE!
THE ONE THING I DO KNOW IS THAT "HE" DECEIVED ME.
THEN -
WHY DO YOU STAY?
!

WHY NOT LEAVE THIS INSANE CITY?
LAHTI...
HE STARTLED ME... FOR A SECOND, I THOUGHT HE WAS COYOTE.
THEY HAVE THE SAME AURA.
...THE AURA OF MEN WHO HAVE BEEN HARDENED BY BATTLE.
IF YOU DON'T LIKE IT HERE, YOU SHOULD COME TO MY TOWN.
YOU'RE WAITING, AREN'T YOU? ...FOR COYOTE.

STUB-BORN, AREN'T YOU?
...I'M NOT WAITING FOR THAT JERK!
YOU'RE THE ONE WHO'S WAITING -
FOR KAI, WHO WAS ABDUCTED!
NO... I'M NOT WAITING AROUND, EITHER.
HUH?
I'M GOING TO GET HIM BACK -
EVEN IF IT MEANS KILLING YOUR PRECIOUS COYOTE.
BUT I NEEDED TO KNOW MORE ABOUT THE OTHER SIDE...
AND I DISCOVERED SOMETHING INTERESTING WHILE DIGGING FOR INFO ON "ISIS."
"SOME-THING INTEREST-ING?"
CLAK

CLIK

OOH, WHAT'S THIS?
RABBLE
RABBLE
I'VE NEVER SEEN ANYTHING LIKE IT, EITHER.
IT'S OLD - AND REQUIRES AN OLD METHOD TO ACCESS IT.
GIVE IT HERE.

mo
THIS DISC IS FROM 100 YEARS AGO.
IT CONTAINS A RECORD OF WHEN "ISIS," THE MOTHER COMPUTER ON THE MOON, WAS CREATED.
...
...
...
HERE.
GLENBACH, SEIKEI
AMADA, TE
ASHVIN, KE
CLIK
CLIK

THESE ARE...?
THE FOUR RESEARCHERS WHO DEVELOPED ISIS.
WHAT'S MORE, YOU THREE ARE APPARENTLY THEIR BLOOD DESCENDANTS.
ASHVIN, KESHINI
AMADA, TETSUYA
GLENBACH, SEIKEI
AND THE LAST ONE IS...

HERMES?!
DEROS, ECHION
– HIS ANCESTOR, I WOULD PRESUME.
HE LIKELY GATHERED YOU THREE TOGETHER, KNOWING OF YOUR BLOODLINES FROM THE BEGINNING.
I'M GUESSING HE NEEDED YOUR DNA TO ACCESS THE ACTUAL "ISIS" UNIT.
IN ORDER TO WAKE "ISIS"...?
THAT'S RIGHT.

SO EVERYTHING WAS A SET-UP RIGHT FROM THE START...
DAMN!
WHY...? WHAT'S THEIR MOTIVE FOR WAKING SOMETHING LIKE THAT?!
THAT'S THE BIG QUESTION.
AS YET, NOTHING SEEMS TO HAVE CHANGED SINCE THE DAY ISIS WAS WOKEN UP FROM HER SLUMBER.
THE MOON IS JUST WATCHING.
I DON'T KNOW WHAT THEY'RE UP TO...
BUT IF THEY'RE NOT GOING TO MOVE, WE'LL JUST HAVE TO LURE THEM OUT.
NOZOMI -
COME WITH ME.
WHAT?!

WITH YOU? NOW?
BUT I'VE GOT TO MAKE DINNER FOR THESE TWO...
I'VE BROUGHT SOMEONE TO TAKE YOUR PLACE.
SHIKI!
HELLO!
CREAK
FINALLY!
I THOUGHT YOU'D NEVER CALL FOR ME, BOSS.
WHAAAT? WHO'S THIS LAME-LOOKING GUY?
CAN HE REALLY COOK?
I'D RATHER HAVE NOZOMI...
WHAT DID YOU SAY?!
DON'T JUDGE A BOOK BY ITS COVER. HE'S ONE OF OUR TOP FOUR OFFICERS.
I LEAVE THINGS HERE TO YOU, SHIKI.
OK, OK.
NOZOMI.
LET'S GO.

HO-HO!
FROM THE LOOKS OF IT, NOZOMI'S GOING OFF TO SHACK UP WITH LAHTI SOMEWHERE.
WE'RE BOTH BEING CHEATED ON!
DOES IT BOTHER YOU, KAI?
...NOT REALLY.
YOU'RE THE ONE WHO SHOULD BE WORRIED.
NOZOMI PROBABLY HATES YOU RIGHT NOW.
CLAK
...PROB-ABLY.
BUT I WAS PRE-PARED FOR IT.

LONELY, ISN'T IT? WANNA GET TOGETHER TO DO SOMETHING GOOD, TOO?
...YOU DON'T MEAN THAT.
I'VE FELT YOUR HOSTILITY EVER SINCE YOU CAME IN.
YOU'RE A SOLDIER, COYOTE.
AM I RIGHT?
HEH.
WHAT A SHARP BOY YOU ARE.
TOO BAD YOU'RE LAHTI'S RIGHT-HAND MAN.
WHAT HAVE YOU PEOPLE BEEN DOING HERE THESE LAST THREE WEEKS? WHERE IS THIS PLACE?
THAT'S ENOUGH!
ASKING TOO MANY QUESTIONS MAY BE HAZARDOUS TO YOUR HEALTH.

SHUT UP.
THAT IS, IF YOU WANT TO GET BACK TO LAHTI.
GRIP
TRUST ME... I WANT TO RETURN YOU SAFELY TO HIM.
THAT'S NO LIE.
CLIK CLAK
FLICKER
SO, BE A GOOD BOY...
AND JUST WATCH SOME TV.

IN THE UPCOMING ELECTION,
THE PROBABILITY THAT INCUMBENT PRESIDENT LESSINOS WILL BE RE-ELECTED IS VERY HIGH.
HOWEVER, CHALLENGING CANDIDATE BERNARDINO IS EXPECTED TO GIVE HIM A GOOD FIGHT.
NOW, HERE IS A GRAPH SHOWING THE CURRENT...
... ... LAHTI...

I...
...WISH I COULD RETURN, TOO.
I WONDER - IS HE UP THERE ON THE MOON RIGHT NOW?
I DON'T FEEL THE MOON'S GAZE AS STRONGLY HERE AS I DID LAST TIME.

IS HE UP THERE...
LOOKING AT ME EVEN NOW?
COYOTE, THE TRAITOR -
I DON'T BELIEVE HIS WORDS OF LOVE TO ME.
BUT -
I SEE THE MOON'S IN ITS FIRST QUARTER.
LAHTI...
IT'S BEEN QUITE A WHILE SINCE MAN FIRST SET FOOT ON THE MOON.
BUT IT'S NOT YET A PLACE THE GENERAL PUBLIC CAN EASILY VISIT.
WHAT DO YOU THINK, NOZOMI?
DO YOU THINK COYOTE AND THE OTHERS ARE UP THERE ON THE MOON?

I DON'T REALLY KNOW, BUT...
...I WOULDN'T BE SURPRISED IF THEY ARE.
THEY SEEMED LIKE THEY WOULD'VE HAD THE RESOURCES.
I AGREE.
BUT IF THEY ARE ON THE MOON, THAT MEANS WE'LL HAVE TO MAKE THEM COME BACK DOWN.

...?
WELL, YEAH. I CAME HERE TO HELP YOU WITH THAT, RIGHT?
YES.
AND AFTER A LOT OF THINKING, I'VE DECIDED THIS IS THE MOST EFFECTIVE WAY TO LURE THEM.
CLAK
DIE FOR US -
NOZOMI.

LET US KILL YOU.
BEEP..
BEEP..
BEEP..!!
?!
WHAT THE - ?!

WHAT'S WRONG, HERMES?
I DON'T KNOW.
A POWERFUL DIGITAL SIGNAL IS INTERFERING.
DAMMIT! AND WE DON'T HAVE A MINUTE TO SPARE –

! I'VE CAUGHT IT!
DISPLAYING THE IMAGE NOW –
ZZT...

N-...
NOZOMI...?

HE'S...
BEEN KILLED ...?

NO...
NO WAY...
THIS HAS TO BE A *FAKE* IMAGE –
IT'S REAL.
HIS EXPRESSION –
THAT'S THE FACE OF A CORPSE.

LAHTI!
BAM!
OH!
HEY! COYOTE!

WHERE ARE YOU GOING?! COME BACK!
DON'T ABANDON YOUR DUTY! COYOTE!!
LAHTI!!

AHHH!
RUN, LAHTI!
IT'S A RAID...
WHAP!
...GAH!
THUD
...THAT WAS AWFULLY QUICK.
SO -
WERE YOU HIDING SOMEWHERE NEARBY?

I'M GLAD I DIDN'T HAVE TO WAIT VERY LONG...
COYOTE.
LAHTI -
YOU - !

WHOOSH!
WHY?!
WHY DID YOU KILL NOZOMI?!
WHAP
WHOA!
WHACK
HE WAS JUST AN INNOCENT VICTIM!
FWSH
I TRICKED HIM INTO THIS!
KRAK

THUMP!
AND YET...!
THWAP!
HOW DARE YOU!
YOU KILLED *MY* NOZOMI!

ガチ
CLICK
HEAR THAT?
HE CALLED YOU "HIS NOZOMI."
DOES THAT MAKE YOU HAPPY...
...NOZOMI?

...NOZO... MI?
YOU -...
YOU'RE ALIVE...?
S...

KRAK
THUD
YIKES -
YOU REALLY WHACKED HIM HARD.
OUCH!
DON'T KILL HIM, NOZOMI.
OH, I WON'T KILL HIM.
THE STUPID FOOL -

WHAT DO YOU MEAN...
..."MY" NOZOMI...?
YOU JERK...!

HE STOPPED MOVING.
ARE YOU TELLING ME HE WAS TAKEN DOWN?
RIGHT AS WE ARE RUNNING OUT OF TIME -

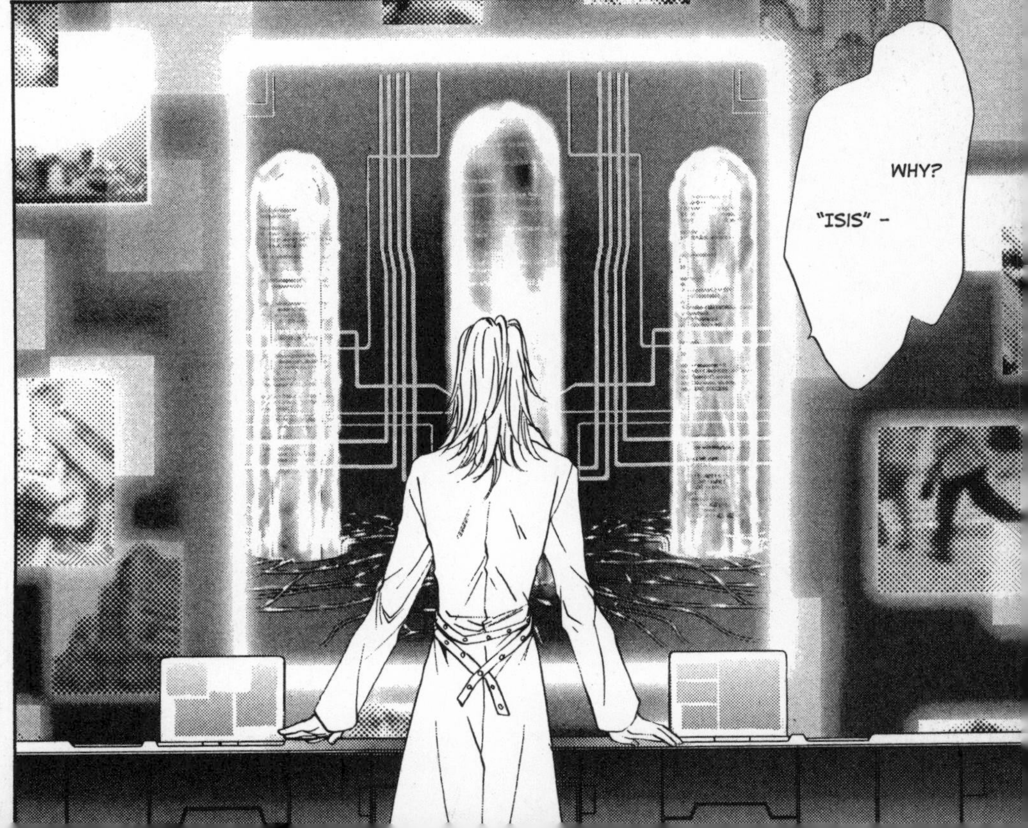
WHY?
"ISIS" -

PLEASE –
LET "OSIRIS" DIE ALREADY.
IF THIS IS YOUR "LOVE"...
IT'S JUST GETTING IN THE WAY.

TAKE COYOTE.

WE'RE GOING TO HAVE HIM TELL US - EVERY-THING.
Steal Moon # 5 / END

StealMoon
スティール ムーン
#6

AS I EXPECTED -
NO CONVENTIONAL MEANS OF PERSUASION WILL MAKE HIM TALK.
IT'S HOW HE'S BEEN TRAINED.
CLIK
CLAK
I'M GUESSING HE'S EITHER MILITARY OR INTELLIGENCE.
CLAK
WE CAN'T WASTE MORE TIME.
CREAK
GET IT OUT OF HIM.
I LEAVE HIM UP TO YOU...
NOZOMI.

WE NEED TO KNOW THEIR MOTIVES.
I'LL LOCK THIS DOOR, BUT I'LL CUT OFF THE SURVEILLANCE MONITORS FOR YOU.

SLAM
...
YO.
I'M HAPPY TO SEE YOU ALIVE, NOZOMI.
WHEN I SAW THAT FOOTAGE, I REALLY THOUGHT YOU WERE DEAD. THE LIFE WAS TOTALLY GONE FROM YOUR FACE.
WAS IT A SPECIAL EFFECT? WHOEVER DID IT WAS *REALLY* INTO CORPSES, I'LL TELL YOU THAT.
... ...
CLAK
BUT NOW I SUPPOSE IT'S *MY* TURN TO BE TURNED INTO A CORPSE...
OH?
YANK

NOZ-...
ピチャッ
SLURP...
!
BITE!
パタタッ
DRIP...
OW -...

OUCH...
PRETTY ANGRY, HUH...?

PEH
OF COURSE.

YOU BETRAYED AND ABANDONED ME.
DON'T THINK YOU'RE GETTING AWAY WITH IT!
I NEVER ABANDONED YOU...THOUGH I ADMIT THE BETRAYING PART.
SHUT UP!
NOW I'M GOING TO MAKE YOU TELL ME...
...THE REASON FOR YOUR BETRAYAL.

...HALF A DAY HAS PASSED ALREADY.
HMM... COYOTE'S SITUATION MUST PREVENT HIM FROM RETURNING.
...I SUPPOSE IT CAN'T BE HELPED.

GRRAK

?
KAI?

CRASH!
?!
KAI...!
GRAB!
GRIP
IF YOU DON'T WANT TO DIE...
TAKE THESE HANDCUFFS OFF OF ME AND LET ME GO.
...AND IF I SAY NO?
I'LL KILL YOU AND SET MYSELF FREE.

THAT... WOULDN'T DO.
CLIK
A...
ARRGHH!
BZZT
BZZT
BZZT
THUD
THE INSIDE OF THOSE CUFFS...
ARE WIRED TO ADMINISTER SHOCK.
DON'T WORRY, IT'S NOT ENOUGH TO KILL YOU.
I'M SORRY...
I CAN'T HAVE YOU LEAVING JUST YET.
THANKS TO COYOTE AND HIS SELFISH WHIMS...

...IT LOOKS LIKE WE'LL HAVE NEED OF YOU.
SUCK
SLURP
SUCK
...! HEY...
NOZOMI –
SLURP
.....
HEY!
MM...

WHAT IS IT...?
YOU MAKE TOO MUCH NOISE.
WHEN DID YOU LEARN TO -
NO, WHAT I MEAN IS -
WHAT ARE YOU DOING...?
WHAT DO YOU MEAN ?
I'M TOR-TURING YOU.
BUT THIS IS JUST MAKING ME FEEL GOOD, ISN'T IT?
OH?
ゆら
SWAY...
SO YOU ADMIT...
IT FEELS GOOD?
TCH!
THAT'S A DAMN SEXY LOOK ON YOUR FACE.

MOVE YOUR BODY A BIT CLOSER.
LET ME LICK YOU, TOO.

SLIP
!
CLINK!

NOZOMI!
TELL ME -
WHAT ARE YOU GUYS UP TO?

WAKING THE SLUMBERING COMPUTER ON THE MOON -
MAKING IT WATCH OVER THIS CITY -
GLOOP...

NN...!
チュク
SQUELCH
I SEE...
NOW, THIS... *IS* TORTURE.
TALK...
...IF YOU WANT ME.

YOU GONNA WITHHOLD IT FROM ME...
'TIL I DO?
IF YOU DON'T TELL ME,
THIS WILL BE OUR LAST TIME.
I'LL FORGET ABOUT YOU AND LEAVE THIS TOWN.
I DON'T GIVE A DAMN ABOUT THE LUNAR COMPUTER –
BUT YOU –
I...

I...
DON'T WANT TO FORGET YOU...
I DON'T CARE WHAT YOU'RE DOING...
I JUST WANT TO BE WITH YOU...!
COME BACK, COYOTE.
COME BACK TO ME!

COYOTE...!!
...
...
SIGH...
I SURRENDER.
...
WHAT?
I SURRENDER. THOUGH I DO FEEL BAD FOR HERMES...
BUT HOW CAN I RESIST YOU WHEN YOU'RE LIKE THIS?
SO, NOZOMI -

HURRY AND WELCOME ME IN.
SQUELCH
UNNH...!
UHH...
OH...!
NN...!

HUFF
UNNH –...!
COYOTE ...
I... I CAN'T MOVE WELL...
HOLD ON –
I'LL DO THE MOVING.
SHOVE
UHH!
CLANK
CLINK
NNGH...
UHH – !

OH...!
LAHTI -
HE SAID YOU WERE EITHER MILITARY OR INTELLIGENCE.
HA - SAW RIGHT THROUGH ME, HUH?
...IT'S TRUE. I'M A SOLDIER.
HERMES AND I CAME TO THIS CITY ON A MISSION.
WE HAD TO FIND YOU, SOMA AND GYOKUTO...
AND WAKE "ISIS" ON THE MOON.
FOR WHAT REASON ?
SHH! KEEP YOUR VOICE DOWN.

"ISIS" IS LISTENING.
GIMME YOUR EAR.
CHOMP
OW!
WHISPER
OUR MOTIVE IS TO WAKE THE SLUMBERING "ISIS"...
SO THAT WE MAY DESTROY HER.
DESTROY "ISIS"...?
THAT'S RIGHT - TO ERASE HER PROGRAMMING AND PUT HER IN ETERNAL SLEEP.
WHY?

BECAUSE –
KCHAK
SORRY TO INTERRUPT, YOU TWO.
IT'S TIME TO COME OUT.
WE'VE BEEN CONTACTED BY HERMES.
HE WANTS TO NEGOTIATE.

SIGH!
I GUESSED AS MUCH.
I DON'T KNOW WHETHER YOU'VE LOST YOUR TOUCH OR YOUR MIND –
BUT I'M DISAPPOINTED IN YOU, COYOTE.
YEAH, I DIDN'T EXPECT THIS, EITHER.
I GUESS LOVE REALLY **DOES** MAKE YOU BLIND.
WHAT ARE YOU TALKING ABOUT?
I DON'T WANT TO HEAR IT.
ANYWAY, HURRY UP AND GET BACK HERE.
LAHTI BARA, I NEED YOU TO RELEASE COYOTE IMMEDI-ATELY.
WHAT ARE YOUR TERMS?
...KAI'S RELEASE.

AH, THAT'S EASY ENOUGH –
– IS WHAT I'D LIKE TO SAY.
BUT I WOULD RATHER HEAR THE REASON BEHIND EVERYTHING THAT'S HAPPENED SO FAR.

I DON'T KNOW WHAT MOTIVE YOU ARE WORKING TOWARD,
BUT YOU *WILL* TAKE RESPON-SIBILITY FOR GETTING THIS ENTIRE CITY INVOLVED.
DEPENDING ON WHAT I HEAR, I MAY EVEN BE WILLING TO LEND YOU A HAND...
IF IT MEANS ENDING THIS RIDICULOUS SITUATION.

...SO, YOU'RE PUTTING KAI'S SAFETY ON THE BACK BURNER?
I'M THIS CITY'S BOSS.
HE KNOWS THAT.
DOES HE ALSO KNOW WHAT A COLD MAN YOU ARE?
DON'T UNDER-ESTIMATE US.

HE HAS ABSOLUTE TRUST IN WHAT I DO.
I KNOW HIM.
THAT'S HOW IT IS BETWEEN US.
"I'M GOING TO GET KAI BACK... EVEN IF IT MEANS KILLING YOUR PRECIOUS COYOTE."
HE PUTS UP A STRONG FRONT... BUT I KNOW WHAT HE SAID TO ME IS TRUE.
- LET'S TELL THEM, HERMES.

COYOTE ?!

LET'S TELL THEM EVERYTHING AND ASK FOR THEIR HELP.
WE CAN'T ACCOMPLISH ANYTHING MORE BY OURSELVES ANYWAY.
AND WE'VE ONLY GOT FIVE DAYS LEFT.
...I SUPPOSE IT CAN'T BE HELPED.
BUT IF WE TALK, IT MUST BE IN A PERFECTLY SOUND-PROOF ROOM...
...SO THAT "ISIS" WILL NOT OVERHEAR.
YOU SEE, "ISIS"...

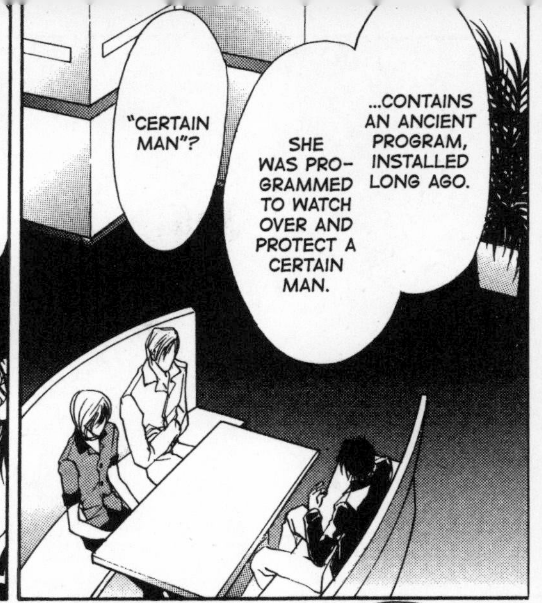
...CONTAINS AN ANCIENT PROGRAM, INSTALLED LONG AGO.
SHE WAS PRO-GRAMMED TO WATCH OVER AND PROTECT A CERTAIN MAN.
"CERTAIN MAN"?

A MAN WHO LIVED IN THIS CITY ONE HUNDRED YEARS AGO -
THE MAN WHO WAS PRE-SIDENT OF THE FEDERA-TION.

KNOWN AS A POLITICIAN OF MATCHLESS AND UNPRECEDENTED ABILITY, HIS LIFE WAS IN CONSTANT DANGER FROM THOSE WHO SOUGHT TO GET HIM OUT OF THE WAY.
SO, IN ORDER TO PROTECT HIM FROM HARM, HIS SUPPORTERS CREATED THIS PROGRAM - "ISIS."
AFTER THE MAN'S DEATH, "ISIS" WENT INTO A LONG SLUMBER.
HOWEVER, IN RECENT YEARS, THERE APPEARED AN ORGANIZATION SEEKING TO CONTROL THIS PROGRAM ANEW.
AFTER SOMEHOW GAINING ILLEGAL ACCESS, A NEW CODE WITH A DIFFERENT DIRECTIVE WAS IMPLEMENTED IN "ISIS" -
A DIRECTIVE TO ATTACK THE VERY MAN SHE HAD LONG BEEN PROGRAMMED TO DEFEND.
WAIT!
HOLD ON A SECOND!

ATTACK THIS MAN...?
BUT HE'S BEEN DEAD FOR A HUNDRED YEARS... *RIGHT?!*
IT'S TRUE.
BUT "ISIS" WAS ABLE TO TRACE THE MAN'S DNA AND LOCK ON TO HIS DESCENDANT.
AND THAT DESCEN-DANT...
...IS THE CURRENT PRESIDENT OF THE FEDERATION, LESSINOS?
THE CURRENT PRESIDENT ?!
...THAT'S RIGHT.
SO THAT'S WHY THERE ARE "ONLY FIVE DAYS LEFT" -
SOMETHING IS SET TO HAPPEN ON ELECTION DAY.
RIGHT. WE MUST ERASE THE "ISIS" PROGRAM FROM THE MAIN COMPUTER BEFORE THAT DEADLINE.
BUT WE'VE ENCOUNTERED AN UNFORESEEN PROBLEM.

IN ORDER TO DELETE "ISIS," WE FOUND OUT THAT WE MUST ALSO DELETE A SUPPORT PROGRAM CALLED "OSIRIS."
BUT THIS PROGRAM HAS PROVED IMPOSSI-BLE TO ERASE.
NO MATTER HOW MANY TIMES "OSIRIS" IS DELETED, "ISIS" ALWAYS RESTORES IT.
AH, ISIS RESUR-RECTING HER HUSBAND.
WHAT?
IT'S FROM ANCIENT MYTHOL-OGY.
THE STORY GOES THAT HER HUSBAND OSIRIS IS KILLED AND HIS CORPSE DISMEMBERED, BUT THE GODDESS ISIS FINDS AND BRINGS HIM BACK TO LIFE.
SHE SEARCHES FOR AND GATHERS UP ALL HIS BODY PARTS WHICH HAD BEEN SCATTERED FAR AND WIDE, AND RESURRECTS OSIRIS.
- A TRULY GORY TALE, I MUST SAY.

"ISIS" WAS SET AWAKEN BEFORE PRESIDEN ELECTIC
BUT THAT'S THE EXTENT OF WHAT WE KNOW. WE HAVE NO IDEA WHAT KIND OF ATTACK IS PLANNED.
POSSIBLY AN ELEC-TRONIC HACKING...
OR A PHYSICAL ATTACK USING ITS ON-BOARD LASER...
WHATEVER THE CASE, IF THIS PROGRAM IS ENACTED, YOU CAN BET THE DAMAGE WON'T BE LIMITED TO JUST LESSINOS - IT WILL BE WIDESPREAD AND SEVERE.
MY GOD...
A CATAS-TROPHE.
CLATTER
ARE YOU SURE THERE ARE REALLY ONLY FIVE DAYS LEFT?!
UNTIL THAT HAPPENS ...?
NOZOMI...

HOW DID YOU EVER THINK -
THE TWO OF YOU COULD STOP A DISASTER LIKE THIS?!
YOU SHOULD HAVE COME CRYING TO ME SOONER -
YOU IDIOT!
I MEAN, IT'S TRUE I MAY NOT HAVE BEEN ABLE TO DO ANYTHING TO HELP, BUT...
SO EMBARRASSING!
...YOU COULD HAVE AT LEAST TALKED TO ME ABOUT IT!
OR WHATEVER...
MAN, I SURE HAVE GOOD TASTE.
I LOVE YA, NOZOMI.
WHA- ...!
WHY ARE YOU ALWAYS SO -...?!
WANNA KISS?

- WELL?
WHAT ABOUT YOU, LAHTI?
YOU GONNA BELIEVE ME...
AND LEND US A HAND?

PIP
...IT LOOKS LIKE I HAVE NO CHOICE BUT TO BELIEVE YOU.

GRRAAK
I DO HAVE SOMEONE WHO MIGHT BE ABLE TO HELP YOU.
SHE'S THE ONE WHO DOCTORED THE IMAGE OF NOZOMI'S DEATH.
WHAT?
SHE SHOULD BE ABLE TO ASSIST IN ANY COMPUTER MATTERS.

HER NAME'S BIHAAN.
SHE'S MY YOUNGER SISTER -
AND...

...KAI'S FORMER LOVER.

Steal Moon#6/ END

HER NAME'S BIHAAN. SHE'S MY YOUNGER SISTER, AND...
...KAI'S FORMER LOVER.
...HUH.
I'D ALWAYS THOUGHT IT WAS KAI AND LAHTI WHO WERE LOVERS, BUT...
!
- WE'RE HERE.
THAT'S OUR HIDEOUT.

IT'S NOWHERE NEAR THE MOON, BUT...
Steal Moon
スティールムーン
#7

WELCOME BACK, COYOTE.
- AND...
LONG-TIME-NO-SEE, NOZOMI.
STOMP STOMP
HERRR-MEEEES...
HOW DARE YOU TRICK ME!!
NOW, NOW, DON'T GET MAD - IT'S ALL BEEN EXPLAINED TO YOU, RIGHT?
YEAH, BUT STILL!
I WASN'T HAPPY ABOUT DUPING YOU GUYS EITHER, BUT I HAD MY ORDERS.
I APOLOGIZE, OKAY?
...THE BASEMENT OF AN ABAN-DONED BUILDING...
IT'S A GOOD STRUCTURE - SHIELDED TO BLOCK ELECTRONIC SIGNALS.
AND THEY'VE CHOSEN A LOCATION BETWEEN TERMINALS, WHERE THE SIGNALS DON'T CROSS OVER AND ARE WEAK.

YOU SEEM TO KNOW YOUR STUFF!
SO, YOU'RE LAHTI'S YOUNGER SISTER?
MY NAME IS BIHAAN.
I'LL DO WHATEVER I CAN TO ASSIST.
THAT WOULD BE MOST HELPFUL.
PLEASE... HURRY AND RELEASE KAI.
THAT IS MY ONLY DEMAND.
I ASK FOR NOTHING ELSE.

THEN PLEASE -
COME THIS WAY.

THEY'VE COME TO GET YOU, KAI.
LAHTI...
AND –
MARIA...?!
IT'S BEEN A WHILE.

WHAT ARE *YOU* DOING HERE...?
SHE AGREED TO HELP THESE MEN ON THE CONDITION YOU ARE RELEASED.
GRRAK
ME...?

YOU'RE FREE TO GO.
I'M SORRY WE HAD TO PUT YOU THROUGH THIS, KAI.
PIP

MARIA...

WELL, WE'VE KEPT OUR END OF THE BARGAIN.
THANK YOU.
NOW, IF YOU'LL SHOW ME TO YOUR SYSTEMS ROOM...

WAIT -...
YOU REST AWHILE.
LAHTI -
BUT...

YOU NEEDN'T WORRY.
I'LL GO WITH HER.
NOZOMI –
TAKE KAI SOMEPLACE WHERE HE CAN REST, WILL YOU?
SURE.
HE CAN USE THIS ROOM OVER HERE.

TAP...
THANKS.
......
I'M SUR-PRISED.

I ALWAYS THOUGHT LAHTI WAS MORE SEVERE, BUT...
HE'S ACTUALLY QUITE KIND. LIKE HOW HE WORRIED ABOUT YOU, KAI...
...AND NOW ACCOMPANYING HIS SISTER LIKE THAT.
IT'S NOT THAT HE'S WORRIED FOR MARIA'S SAFETY, IT'S -
?
COME TO THINK OF IT, WHY DO YOU CALL HER MARIA? IS IT A NICKNAME?
NO...
IT'S A NAME OUT OF MY PAST... LONG AGO.
...I SEE.
NOZOMI, I'M GONNA GO CHECK UP ON THINGS.
OH, OKAY.
I'M A LITTLE WORRIED MYSELF.

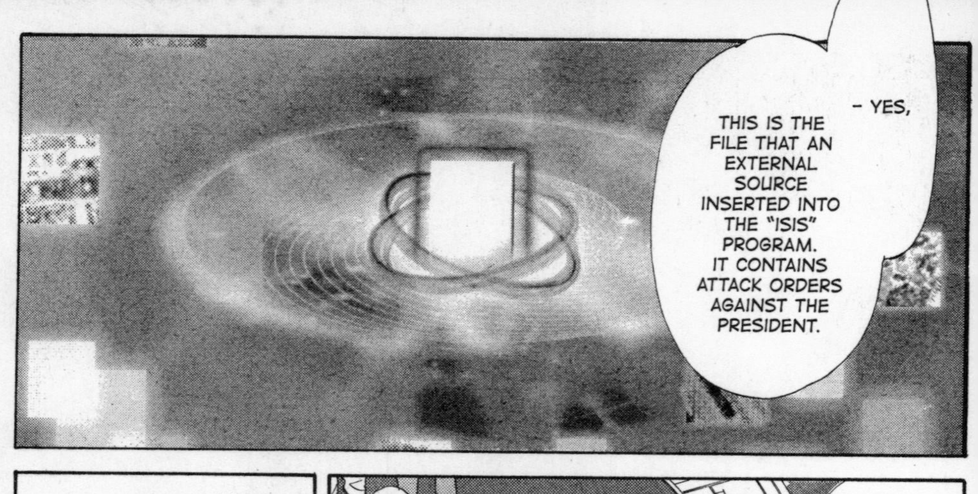
- YES,
THIS IS THE FILE THAT AN EXTERNAL SOURCE INSERTED INTO THE "ISIS" PROGRAM. IT CONTAINS ATTACK ORDERS AGAINST THE PRESIDENT.

IT APPEARS THE PROGRAM IS SET TO ACTIVATE ON ELECTION DAY.
THOSE THINGS AROUND IT ARE PROTECTION PROGRAMS DESIGNED TO HAMPER INTERFERENCE. THEY'RE QUITE STRONG, AND WE CAN'T GET AROUND THEM.
...I SEE.
DO YOU THINK YOU CAN DO SOMETHING ABOUT THEM?
I'LL TRY.
- WHAT ARE YOU READING?

OH, JUST THIS BOOK I FOUND.
I THINK IT BELONGS TO HERMES. IT'S ALL ABOUT ANCIENT MYTHOLOGY.
ARE YOU INTERESTED IN SUCH THINGS?
NO, NOT REALLY - BUT...
I HEARD THAT "ISIS" IS A NAME TAKEN FROM ANCIENT MYTHOLOGY, SO...
OH, HERE - LOOK!
"ISIS" -
Isis
"A GODDESS OF ANCIENT EGYPT, SHE IS THE DAUGHTER OF GEB, GOD OF EARTH, AND NUT, GODDESS OF SKY.
HER SIBLINGS, ALSO BORN FROM NUT, ARE OSIRIS, SET, NEPHTHYS AND HAROERIS.
ISIS BECOMES HER BROTHER OSIRIS'S WIFE, BUT OSIRIS IS KILLED AND DISMEMBERED BY THEIR OTHER BROTHER, SET.
ISIS FINDS AND GATHERS ALL OF HER HUSBAND'S SCATTERED BODY PARTS AND, USING HER MAGIC, BRINGS HIM BACK TO LIFE. SHE IS ONE OF THE GODS OF THE NINE (OR MAIN) PILLARS..." - SO IT SAYS.

...I DON'T REALLY UNDERSTAND IT TOO WELL, BUT IT SOUNDS TERRIFYING.
THEY WERE KILLING EACH OTHER, EVEN THOUGH THEY WERE SIBLINGS?
SEEMS LIKE IT... OH! LOOK!
"ISIS RECEIVED ASSISTANCE FROM THE GOD THOTH.
THOTH IS ALSO REFERRED TO AS HIS GREEK EQUIVALENT, HERMES, AND IS KNOWN AS THE GOD OF MAGIC AND ALCHEMY, AS WELL AS THE DEITY OF THE MOON."
AH!
SO *THAT'S* WHERE HERMES TOOK HIS NAME FROM!
UGH, IT'S ALL SO WEIRD.
HAHA...
EEEEEEE
HA...
?
KAI?

WHAT'S WRONG?
KAI?
KAI?!
WHAT'S THE MATTER?
...NO...

ガタ
CLATTER
NO...
LAHTI...!!
HUH?!
KAI?!
DASH!
KAI!!

AMAZING! SHE REALLY DISMANTLED THE PROTECTION PROGRAMS WITHOUT "ISIS" NOTICING.
... YEAH.
RIGHT NOW, I'M OVER-WRITING THE CODE WITH NEW ORDERS TO STOP THE ATTACK.
AFTER THAT, EVERY-THING SHOULD BE OKAY...
STOMP
STOMP
STOMP
MARIA !!

THWAP!
KAI?! WHAT ARE YOU -...?!
IT'S A TRAP!
SHE HAS NO INTENTION OF DISEN- GAGING THIS PROGRAM!
SHE'S THE ONE WHO CREATED IT IN THE FIRST PLACE!

YOU SEE, INSIDE MY HEAD IS A CHIP SHE IMPLANTED IN ME LONG AGO.
THE CHIP PICKS UP AND RECEIVES ANY DATA CODE SHE CREATES.
I'M CERTAIN OF IT!
CHK
I BELIEVE YOU.
SHE IS A CYBER-TERRORIST.
CHUCKLE
SILLY KAI...

MARIA...
WHY ARE YOU DOING THIS?
IF YOU "DETECTED" THIS CODE, WHY DIDN'T YOU JUST RUN?
I WAS GENER-OUSLY GOING TO LET YOU BE THE ONLY ONE TO ESCAPE...
BECAUSE I WAS HIRED TO - THAT'S ALL.
AND THE ONE WHO HIRED YOU... WAS IT THE OPPOSING PRESIDENTIAL CANDIDATE, BERNARDINO...?
I CAN ONLY SAY THAT I WAS HIRED BY SOMEONE.
THEN WE'LL FORCE IT OUT OF YOU.
B...
CAN YOU, I WONDER...?
?!
WHAT WAS THAT?!
OOOOM
SHK!

KINK!
!!
LAHTI!
WHAP
I SUGGEST YOU HURRY AND RUN, BROTHER.
...OR ELSE BE BURIED ALIVE.

KRAK!
BAM
BAM
RUMBLE...
DON'T, LAHTI! YOU'LL HIT THE COMPUTER SYSTEM!
UH, THAT'S THE LEAST OF OUR TROUBLES.
EVERYONE, RUN!
IT'S A RESULT OF MARIA'S NEW PROGRAM!

"ISIS" IS ATTACKING THIS PLACE!

FLASH!
RUMBLE
RUMBLE

I SWEAR ...
THIS IS ONE UNBELIEVABLE STUNT SHE PULLED...

I APOLOGIZE.
I NEVER GUESSED SHE WAS INVOLVED.
I SHOULD HAVE REALIZED IT THE MOMENT SHE SAID SHE'D HELP.
BUT ANYONE WOULD'VE BELIEVED HER WHEN SHE SAID SHE WANTED TO RESCUE HER LOVER!
BUT THAT'S JUST IT - IT'S THE LAST THING I SHOULD HAVE BELIEVED FROM A WOMAN LIKE HER.
AT ANY RATE, I'M SORRY FOR THE TROUBLE I CAUSED YOU.
PLEASE USE THE SYSTEM HERE HOW YOU LIKE.
WHAT'RE YOU DOING?
PLAY WITH US!
RIGHT NOW, OUR SHIKI IS ATTEMPTING TO DEAL WITH THE FILE BIHAAN ACTIVATED.
SHOULD YOU NEED HIM, HE'S AT YOUR DISPOSAL.
WELL, AT ANY RATE...
LET US REST TODAY.
ME AND NOZOMI WILL TAKE A ROOM - ALL RIGHT?

HOW CAN YOU BE SO LAZY?!
WE ONLY HAVE A FEW DAYS LEFT, RIGHT?!
THAT'S RIGHT, COYOTE. WE NEED TO BORROW THEIR COMMUNI-CATIONS ROOM AND COME UP WITH A PLAN...
HERMES - !
OUR NEXT PLAN...
...IS ALREADY DECIDED. AM I RIGHT?
COME ON, LET'S REST. I'M TIRED.
... ... FINE.
COYOTE...
YOU'RE UP TO SOMETHING AGAIN, AREN'T YOU?

YOU DON'T TRUST ME?
OF COURSE NOT!
BARGING INTO MY BATH...

BUT EVEN IF I TRY TO STOP YOU...
I KNOW YOU'LL JUST GO AND DO SOMETHING DANGEROUS.

...I WON'T DO ANYTHING BAD ANYMORE.
LIAR!
IT'S THE TRUTH.

I...
ONLY WANT TO DO GOOD THINGS WITH YOU FROM NOW ON.
NN...!
NOZOMI -
WHY ARE YOU GUYS STILL WEARING THESE COLLARS?
BITE
...HUH?
BUT IT'S RIGGED TO EXPLODE IF IT'S REMOVED, ISN'T IT?
SPLASH
THAT WAS TURNED OFF LONG AGO.
NO WAY... UNNH ...!
IT'S TRUE.
SPLASH
SPLASH

YOU'RE FREE NOW!
COYOTE ...?
ALTHOUGH –
I WISH I COULD'VE KEPT YOU IMPRISONED FOREVER.
SLIP
NNH!
UHH – !

I REGRET HAVING TO LET YOU GO.
THAT MARIA...
SHE WAS THE SAME AS EVER, WASN'T SHE?
YES.

YOU KNOW...
YOU COULD HAVE TAKEN HER DOWN IF YOU'D AIMED FOR HER NECK.
WHAT ABOUT YOU?
NOT ONE OF YOUR SHOTS HIT HER.
...I SUPPOSE WE BOTH HAVE A WEAK SPOT FOR THAT WOMAN.
I'M SURE WE WERE BOTH JUST TIRED.
PLEASE, REST NOW.
YOU'RE RIGHT.
IT'LL BE OUR FIRST GOOD NIGHT'S SLEEP IN A MONTH.

...YES.

CREAK...

LATER, NOZOMI.
HUH!
...
...
COYOTE ?!
WHY?
...WHAT IS THIS?
I FEEL UNEASY...
BA-BUMP
IS HE...
JUST UP EARLIER THAN ME...?
BA-BUMP
COYOTE ?!

WHY CAN'T I FIND HIM ANYWHERE ?!
COYOTE!

LAHTI!
WHAT'S WRONG, NOZOMI?
WHY ALL THE SHOUTING?

HAVE YOU SEEN COYOTE ANYWHERE?! I CAN'T FIND HIM!
COYOTE?
NO, I HAVEN'T SEEN HIM.

IF YOU'RE LOOKING FOR COYOTE...

...HE'S NO LONGER HERE.

HE LEFT.
... ...
WHAT?!
HE...
LEFT?
WHAT FOR...?
WE MAY NOT BE ABLE TO STOP "ISIS" NOW.
THE PRESIDENTIAL ELECTION IS IN THREE DAYS.
WE'D CONSIDERED A WORST-CASE SCENARIO... AND PREPARED FOR IT.

NOZOMI -
DID YOU KNOW "COYOTE" WAS JUST AN ALIAS?
WELL...
I SUSPECTED IT, BUT...
COYOTE'S REAL NAME IS RÔ WAITS LESSINOS.
!
"LESSINOS" ?!
YES.
HE'S THE ONLY SON OF PRESIDENT LESSINOS.

COYOTE?!
THE PRESIDENT'S SON?!
NOZOMI - COYOTE IS...
WAIT! HOLD ON.
YOU SAID "ISIS" WAS PROGRAMMED TO TRACE LESSINOS' DNA, TRACK HIS DESCENDANT AND ATTACK HIM, RIGHT?
DOES THAT MEAN COYOTE...
YES... IT'S AS YOU GUESS.
YOU SEE -

WHEN COYOTE ACCESSED "ISIS" -
HE OVER-WROTE ALL OF HIS FATHER'S DATA WITH HIS OWN.
HE MADE *HIMSELF* THE TARGET INSTEAD OF HIS FATHER.
RIGHT NOW, HE'S LIKELY HEADED SOMEPLACE DESOLATE, WHERE THERE WILL BE NO OTHER CASUALTIES.

SOMEPLACE EMPTY, ALL ALONE –
TO RECEIVE ISIS' ATTACK...
HE...
I WON'T DO ANYTHING BAD ANYMORE.

I ONLY WANT TO DO GOOD THINGS WITH YOU -
FROM NOW ON.
HOW...
HOW COULD YOU DO THIS, COYOTE?!
DAMMIT...!
I WISH I COULD'VE KEPT YOU IMPRISONED FOREVER.

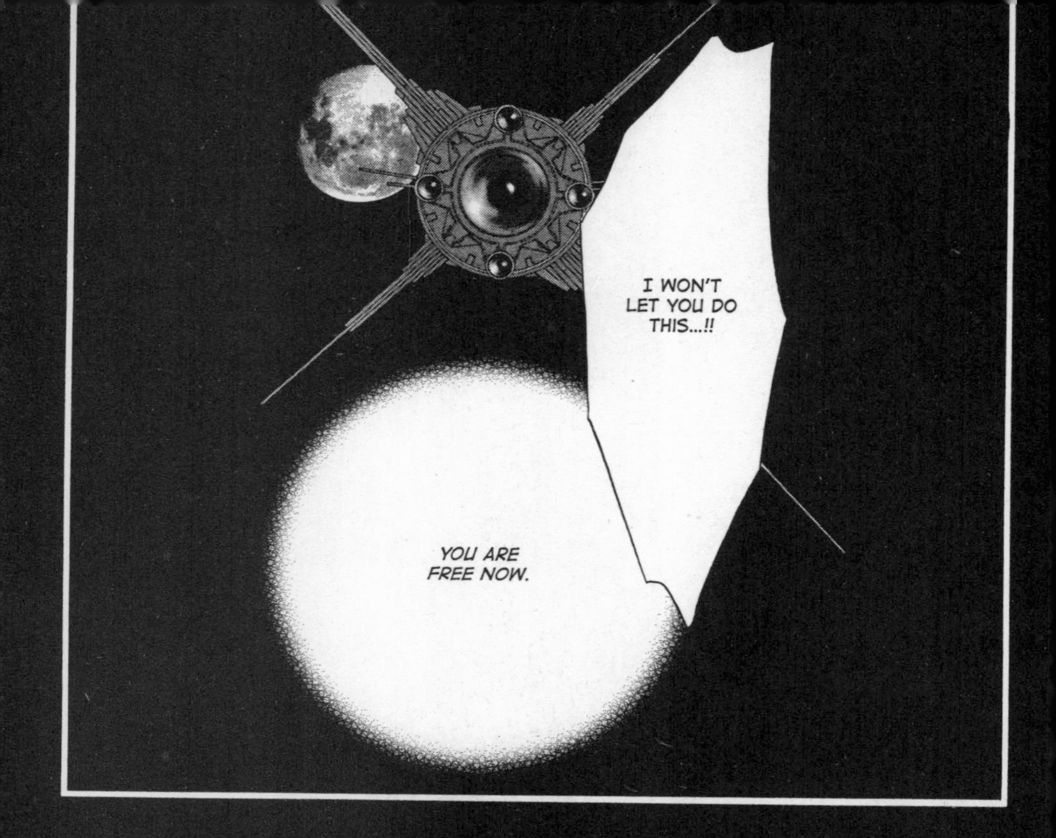

Steal Moon # 7 / END

Steal Moon
スティール ムーン

Steal Moon
スティールムーン
#8

IT TURNS OUT COYOTE -
IS PRESIDENT LESSINOS'S ONLY SON.
BY OVER-WRITING HIS FATHER'S DATA WITH HIS OWN, COYOTE MADE HIMSELF THE TARGET OF "ISIS."
NOW, HE'S LEFT THIS CITY, ALONE, TO SOMEPLACE DESERTED...
TO AWAIT "ISIS" - AND HIS OWN CERTAIN DEATH.
...
HUH?
LATELY...
I DON'T FEEL THE MOON'S GAZE AS MUCH...
THE ATTENTION OF "ISIS" HAS BEEN DIVERTED FROM THIS CITY.

IT LOOKS LIKE COYOTE HAS HEADED FOR THE MOUNTAINS TO THE SOUTH.

I GET IT NOW... THE REASON "ISIS" WAS WATCHING THIS CITY...
WAS BECAUSE COYOTE WAS HERE.

YES. I'D WANTED TO STOP "ISIS" IN THIS CITY, WHERE HER TERMINUS IS LOCATED.
I NEVER WANTED COYOTE TO BE FORCED INTO THIS DECISION.

TWO MORE DAYS HAVE PASSED SINCE THEN, AND WE STILL HAVE NO SOLUTION –
...WHAT TIME IS "ISIS" SET TO ATTACK?
WE DON'T KNOW YET.
FSSHT
I'VE GOT IT!

THE ATTACK PROGRAM IN "ISIS" IS SET TO ACTIVATE AT 9 A.M.!
THE EXACT TIME VOTING FOR THE PRESIDENTIAL ELECTION BEGINS!!
IT'S 00:02 A.M. NOW, WHICH MEANS -
WE'VE ONLY GOT NINE HOURS...!
THAT'S IT...?
NINE HOURS...
WHAT ARE WE SUPPOSED TO DO IN JUST NINE HOURS...?!
ARE WE...
...HELPLESS TO DO ANYTHING BUT LET HIM BE KILLED? MY COYOTE -
SHIVER

MY COYOTE, KILLED BY THAT STUPID THING...!!
NO...
NO! I WON'T LET IT!
HERMES! WHAT CAN I DO?! HOW CAN I KEEP COYOTE FROM DYING?!
NOZOMI ...
EVEN IF WE FIND THAT STUBBORN FOOL, HE'LL REFUSE TO COME BACK, EVEN IF WE DRAG HIM!
WHAT AM I SUPPOSED TO DO? WHAT CAN I -
NOZOMI!
CALM DOWN, NOZOMI!
OH...

GRIP...
...
I CAN'T...
I CAN'T LET HIM DIE OUT THERE ALL ALONE...
I WISH HE'D AT LEAST TAKEN ME WITH HIM.
I CAN'T...!
HE SAID I WAS HIS SERVANT...!
...NOZOMI, I'M SORRY.
I NEVER THOUGHT YOU'D SUFFER SO MUCH,
IT'S ALL OUR FAULT.
..."OUR"?
TO BE COMPLETELY ACCURATE, THE FAULT OF MY AND YOUR ANCESTORS.

NOZOMI... YOUR ANCESTOR, DR. TETSUYA AMADA -
SOMA'S ANCESTOR, DR. KESHINI ASHVIN -
AND GYOKUTO'S ANCESTOR, DR. SEIKEI GLENBACH -
THEY WERE ALL MY COLLEAGUES.
...HERMES?
JUST WHO *ARE* YOU...?
MY REAL NAME IS ECHION DEROS.
I'M ONE OF THE FOUR RESEARCHERS WHO CREATED "ISIS."

CREATED "ISIS"...?
SO THAT'S THE SITUATION, FATHER.
PLEASE DON'T WORRY ABOUT ME. I WISH YOU THE BEST OF LUCK IN THE ELECTION TOMORROW.
MY SON... HOW COULD YOU DO THIS...?
SURELY THE ELECTION IS NOT WORTH LOSING YOU...!
NO -
YOU *MUST* CONTINUE TO HOLD THE OFFICE OF PRESIDENT, FATHER.

...I'LL HAVE INVESTIGA-TIONS INTO BERNARDINO CONTINUED.
DON'T GIVE UP HOPE UNTIL THE VERY END. HAVE YOU ANY REQUESTS...?
I'M A SOLDIER.
I'VE ALWAYS BEEN READY TO GIVE MY LIFE.
THIS WAY, THERE WILL BE NO COLLATERAL DAMAGE. THIS IS HOW IT SHOULD BE.
YES -
JUST ONE.
- THAT'S RIGHT.
AFTER WE CREATED "ISIS," THE FOUR OF US ENTERED CRYOGENIC SLEEP ON THE MOON.
WE NEEDED TO PROTECT AND MAINTAIN THE ACTIVATION KEYWORDS FOR A SET PERIOD OF TIME.

KEY-WORDS?
YES, THE NECESSARY KEYS FOR DEACTIVATING "ISIS" -
A WORD RELATED TO "THE MOON," YOUR LAST NAMES AND YOUR DNA.
IT'S THE REASON ALL OF YOUR NAMES HAVE A CONNECTION TO THE MOON.
THE THREE TERMINI OF "ISIS" - "SELENE," "ARTEMIS," AND "HECATE" -
I SEARCHED FOR THE DESCENDANTS WHO COULD ACCESS THESE TERMINI, AND SECURED YOU AS "DIGITAL ANGELS."
ALL OF THE RESEARCHERS EXCEPT ME WERE MARRIED AND HAD FAMILIES, SO THE NAMING CUSTOM WAS PASSED DOWN.
IF YOUR KEYWORDS WERE ACCESSED TOGETHER WITH MY KEYWORD, "THOTH," WE SHOULD HAVE BEEN ABLE TO STOP "ISIS."
BUT SOMETHING IRREGULAR IS GOING ON INSIDE OF "ISIS."
SHE REFUSES TO ENTER SLEEP, ALMOST AS IF SHE SENSES AN "ENEMY" SOMEWHERE.
...WHAT ABOUT THE GUYS WHO ENTERED COLD SLEEP WITH YOU?
YOU KNOW, OUR ANCESTORS - IF THEY COULD HELP US...
THE OTHERS SEEM TO HAVE AWAKENED BEFORE I DID.
THEY'VE ALL PASSED AWAY NOW.

I SEE...
NO WONDER I'VE NEVER MET THEM BEFORE.
AND HOW OLD ARE YOU EXACTLY, HERMES?!
AT ANY RATE -
LET'S TRY TO ACCESS "ISIS" ONE MORE TIME... NO, AS MANY TIMES AS IT TAKES.
IT'S ALL WE CAN DO...
BEEP -!
BEEP -!

!
AN EMERGENCY COMMUNICATION?!
BEEP -!
BEEP -!

HAS SOMEONE INFILTRATED AGAIN?!

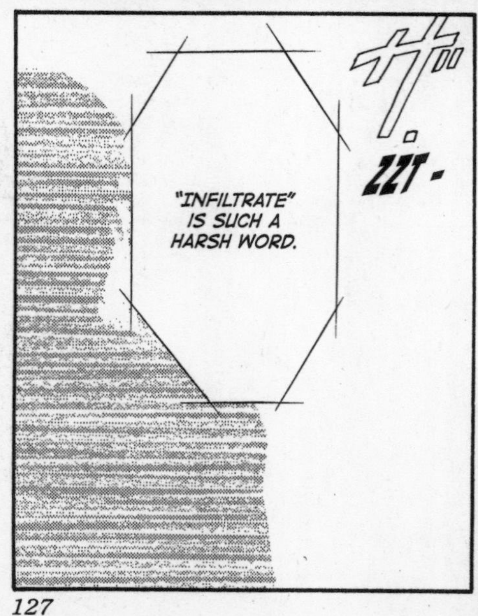
ZZT -
"INFILTRATE" IS SUCH A HARSH WORD.

DON'T YOU THINK SO...
NOZOMI?
...
Y-...

YOU IDIOT!
JUMP!
WHERE THE HELL -
I MEAN - I ALREADY KNOW, BUT...
NOZOMI...
I'M SORRY.

YOU HEARD EVERYTHING, RIGHT?
THAT'S HOW IT IS.
I'M PROBABLY GOING TO DIE.
IT CAN'T BE HELPED.
BUT I COULDN'T HELP SENDING ONE LAST TRANSMISSION.
COYOTE, THIS LINE YOU'RE USING... IS IT -
YEAH - I'M BORROWING MY OLD MAN'S HOTLINE.
THE PRESIDENT'S -...!
ISN'T...
ISN'T THERE SOMETHING YOUR FATHER CAN DO?! BY USING HIS CLOUT OR SOMETHING...
CAN HE SHOOT "ISIS" DOWN WITH ANOTHER SATELLITE, OR MAKE THE GUYS WHO DID THIS CONFESS...?!
IT WOULDN'T WORK.
"ISIS" IS MASSIVE.
CAN YOU IMAGINE THE DEBRIS THAT WOULD RAIN DOWN ON EARTH? AND IF "ISIS" FOUGHT BACK, THE DAMAGE WOULD SPREAD.
HE IS TRYING TO FIND THE CULPRITS BEHIND THIS SCHEME, BUT...
TIME'S UP.

NOZOMI.
THIS PLACE HAS A STRONG MAGNETIC FIELD. IT'S ALSO ROCKY AND BARREN, AND THERE ARE NO TOWNS NEARBY.
ALL THAT'S LEFT IS FOR ME TO DIE HERE, ALONE.
AND I'M FINE WITH THAT.
NO!
I'LL GO THERE, TOO!
I WANT TO DIE THERE WITH YOU!
YOU CAN'T.
COYOTE!
I WON'T ALLOW IT, NOZOMI.
I WON'T ALLOW IT BECAUSE I LOVE YOU.

IF YOU LOVE ME, LIVE.
LIVE AND FORGET ABOUT ME.
IT WAS NEVER MY PLAN TO FALL IN LOVE WITH YOU, BUT...
I'M CONTENT WITH THIS OUTCOME.
ZZT
THE SIGNAL WILL BE CUT SOON.
GOOD-BYE, NOZOMI. I LOVE YOU.
NO...
WAIT!
YOU ALWAYS SAY AND DO WHAT YOU WANT!
NOZOMI!
DON'T GO, COYOTE!
DON'T GO!!

YOU CAN'T DIE - !
SOMEBODY HELP! HELP HIM!
YOU ARE THE ENEMY WHO IS GOING TO KILL THE MAN I LOVE...!
THE ENEMY...
ISIS! YOU ARE MY ENEMY!!
SOMEONE!
NOZOMI...
ARE YOU ALL RIGHT?
NOZOMI?

- ENEMY...?! -

HERMES ...
WHAT IS IT?
WHO DID YOU SAY...
THE ENEMY OF "ISIS" IS...?
HUH?
YOU SAID IT EARLIER - THAT IT'S "AS IF SHE SENSES AN 'ENEMY' SOME- WHERE."
HM, LET'S SEE...THE ENEMY OF THE GODDESS ISIS...
IN MYTHOLOGY, I GUESS THAT WOULD BE SET - THE BROTHER WHO KILLS HER HUSBAND, OSIRIS.
- THAT'S IT.
THAT'S GOT TO BE IT. SOMEHOW -
SOME- WHERE... "SET" EXISTS!

"SET"?!
BUT THERE IS NO SUCH PROGRAM!
IF ONLY WE COULD FIND "SET"...
...WE MIGHT BE ABLE TO STOP "ISIS"!
MAYBE IT'S *NOT* A PROGRAM.
BUT I'M SURE "SET" EXISTS. THAT'S WHY "ISIS" WON'T GO TO SLEEP!
WHAT IF SHE THINKS THE DISAPPEARANCE OF "OSIRIS" IS SOMEHOW "SET'S" DOING, AND SHE'S SEEKING TO RESURRECT "OSIRIS"?!
THINK! WHAT WAS IN THAT BOOK I READ?!
IT WAS ABOUT THE MOTHER AND FATHER OF ISIS... AND HER SIBLINGS.
ISIS HAS FIVE SIBLINGS... TWO OF THEM ARE "SET" AND "OSIRIS" -
...
FIVE...?

COULD IT BE?!
FWSH!
NOZOMI ?!
SOMA! GYOKUTO! COME WITH ME.
HERMES, I NEED YOU TO STAY HERE.
STOMP
COULD IT BE -
STOMP
LAHTI!
STOMP
KAI!
BAM!
NOZOMI?
WHAT'S HAPPENED? HAS THERE BEEN A DEVELOPMENT?
LAHTI, I HAVE A FAVOR TO ASK!
I NEED YOUR HELP!

IF MY SUSPICIONS ARE CORRECT, THEN...!!
PLEASE -
TAKE US TO THE "ISIS" TERMINUS!

WHAT'S SUPPOSED TO BE HERE?
DASH
THIS IS THE "SELENE" TERMINUS -
THE CENTRAL PILLAR IS THE MAIN COMPUTER, AND THE FOUR BEHIND IT ARE THE SUB-COMPUTERS.
IF THESE THINGS ARE WHAT I THINK THEY ARE -
"SET" SHOULD BE HERE!
- I FOUND IT!
NOZOMI!
I FOUND THE NAME! IT'S ON THE BACK!
OVER HERE, TOO!

NAME?
SO I WAS RIGHT!
WHAT DOES IT SAY?!
"NEPHTHYS" –
"HAROERIS" –
カッ
TAP
I FOUND YOU...
..."SET" ...!
SET

WHAT DOES THIS MEAN, NOZOMI?
I'LL EXPLAIN LATER! FOR NOW, TAKE GYOKUTO AND SOMA TO THE TOWNS OF TWILIGHT CITY AND HIGH NOON!
TWILIGHT CITY AND HIGH NOON?
GIVE ME TIME. I'LL CONTACT THEM TO LET THEM KNOW WE'RE COMING FIRST.
A GANG FIGHT COULD BREAK OUT IF WE JUST WALTZ IN UNANNOUNCED...
THERE'S NO TIME, LAHTI!!

WE'VE ONLY GOT FIVE MORE HOURS –
FIVE MORE HOURS UNTIL COYOTE DIES!
HE'S ALREADY GIVEN UP, BUT...
I HAVEN'T! I HAVE TO STOP IT!!
...I WON'T LET IT KILL HIM.

I'M GOING TO GET HIM BACK...!!
...KAI.
YES?
YOU AND SHIKI ACCOMPANY THEM TO HIGH NOON AND TWILIGHT CITY.
TAP
I UNDER-STAND.

YES.
YOU MAY GET A VIOLENT WELCOME.
BE CAREFUL.
SKREEK
SCREECH
NOW -
LET'S HAVE AN EXPLANATION, NOZOMI.

...YEAH.
EVERYONE... PLEASE LISTEN.
RIGHT.
"AKATSUKI," "TWILIGHT CITY," "HIGH NOON" –
THE "ISIS" TERMINI LOCATED IN THESE THREE CITIES ARE IN THE SHAPE OF FIVE PILLARS.
IN EGYPT, IT IS SAID THAT GODS DWELL IN PILLARS.
CALLED THE "MAIN PILLARS," THESE ARE WHAT THE TERMINI REPRESENT.
THE GODDESS ISIS HAS EXACTLY FIVE SIBLINGS.
THEY ARE KNOWN AS THE GODS OF THE MAIN PILLARS.

FROM THE LEFT -
"NEPHTHYS"...
"HAROERIS"...
"ISIS" AT THE CENTER ...
"OSIRIS" ...
AND FINALLY,
"SET" -
I SUSPECT THE MAIN COMPUTER ON THE MOON HAS NOTHING CORRESPONDING TO THESE NAMES.
THESE ARE THE NAMES OF EXTERNAL HARD DRIVES THAT WERE ADDED LATER, TO HANDLE ONE HUNDRED YEARS' WORTH OF ACCUMULATED DATA.
...I SEE.
NO WONDER I DIDN'T KNOW ABOUT THEM.
THAT'S RIGHT.
"ISIS" MUST NOT HAVE KNOWN OF THEM EITHER, AND BECAME CONFUSED.
BUT IS A COMPUTER CAPABLE OF REACTING IN SUCH A HUMAN, EMOTIONAL MANNER?
I DON'T KNOW. IT COULD BE SOME KIND OF ERROR THAT MAKES IT SEEM THAT WAY.

SET
THE TERMINI IN THE OTHER TOWNS PROBABLY HAVE THESE SAME HARD DRIVES ATTACHED, TOO.
BUT MAYBE THE DESIRE TO SAVE SOMEONE YOU LOVE...
EXISTS IN EVERYTHING - EVEN A COMPUTER.
IF WE BREAK THESE, WE MAY BE ABLE TO STOP "ISIS."
HURRY -
PLEASE, HURRY -
GOOD MORNING.
AT LONG LAST, ELECTION DAY IS HERE.
EVERYONE, PLEASE HEAD TO THE VOTING AREAS.
VOTE FOR A REPRE-SENTATIVE OF THE PEOPLE, CHOSEN BY THE PEOPLE!
VROOOM
HEY!

YOU! WHAT CITY ARE YOU FROM?!
HONK -
AT LEAST PAY YOUR RESPECTS!
STOP THE CAR!
HONK -
- SORRY.
S...
BLAM
WHAM!
SKREEK
OOH! NICE ONE!
THERE'LL BE HELL TO PAY LATER...

STOP!
I SAID STOP!
ARE YOU GUYS FROM AKATSUKI TURF?!
SKREEECH

GET DOWN.
DUCK
?!
THWAP!
HUH?!
WHOA -
SLIDE
YANK!
WHOAAA!
THUD!
I'LL GET YOU - !
VROOOM

SLAM!
SLAM!
WE'RE HERE!

WHAT NOW, NOZOMI!?!
HURRY TO THE RESPECTIVE TERMINI!
SEARCH FOR "SET"!
IS IT THERE?!
FOUND IT!
ME, TOO!

GYOKUTO!
SOMA!
TAKE OFF YOUR COLLARS!

REMOVE THEM...
AND PLACE THEM ON TOP OF THE HARD DRIVE LABELED "SET!"
SET
SHIKI!
KAI!
LAHTI!
I NEED YOU THREE TO SHOOT THE COLLARS SIMULTANE-OUSLY!!
3...
2...
1...

SHOOT !!
BLAM!
BZZT!

ズウ
BOOOM!

ジュオオ
FSSHHH...
... HERMES ...

I...
I THINK "SET" HAS BEEN TAKEN CARE OF.
SLUMP...
THANK YOU, NOZOMI.
ONLY 20 MINUTES LEFT...
8:41
THE REST IS UP TO ME NOW.
SQUEEZE
PLEASE -
PLEASE LET US MAKE IT IN TIME - !
"ISIS" -
MY NAME IS "HERMES," ALSO KNOWN AS "THOTH" -
I AM THE GOD OF SORCERY, AND TEMPTER OF THE MOON.
CAN YOU HEAR ME?

- I HEAR YOU -
GUARDIAN "THOTH."
"OSIRIS" HAS NOW ENTERED SLEEP.
HE IS IN NO DANGER OF BEING KILLED BY ANYONE ANYMORE.
ISIS
OSIRIS
NOW, IT IS YOUR TURN TO REST.
YOU MAY SLEEP NOW.
...
SLEEP, "ISIS."
YOU NEED NOT GUARD ANYTHING,
OR ANYONE...
...ANY LONGER.
YOU NEED NOT PROTECT NOR ATTACK.
IT IS ALL OVER.

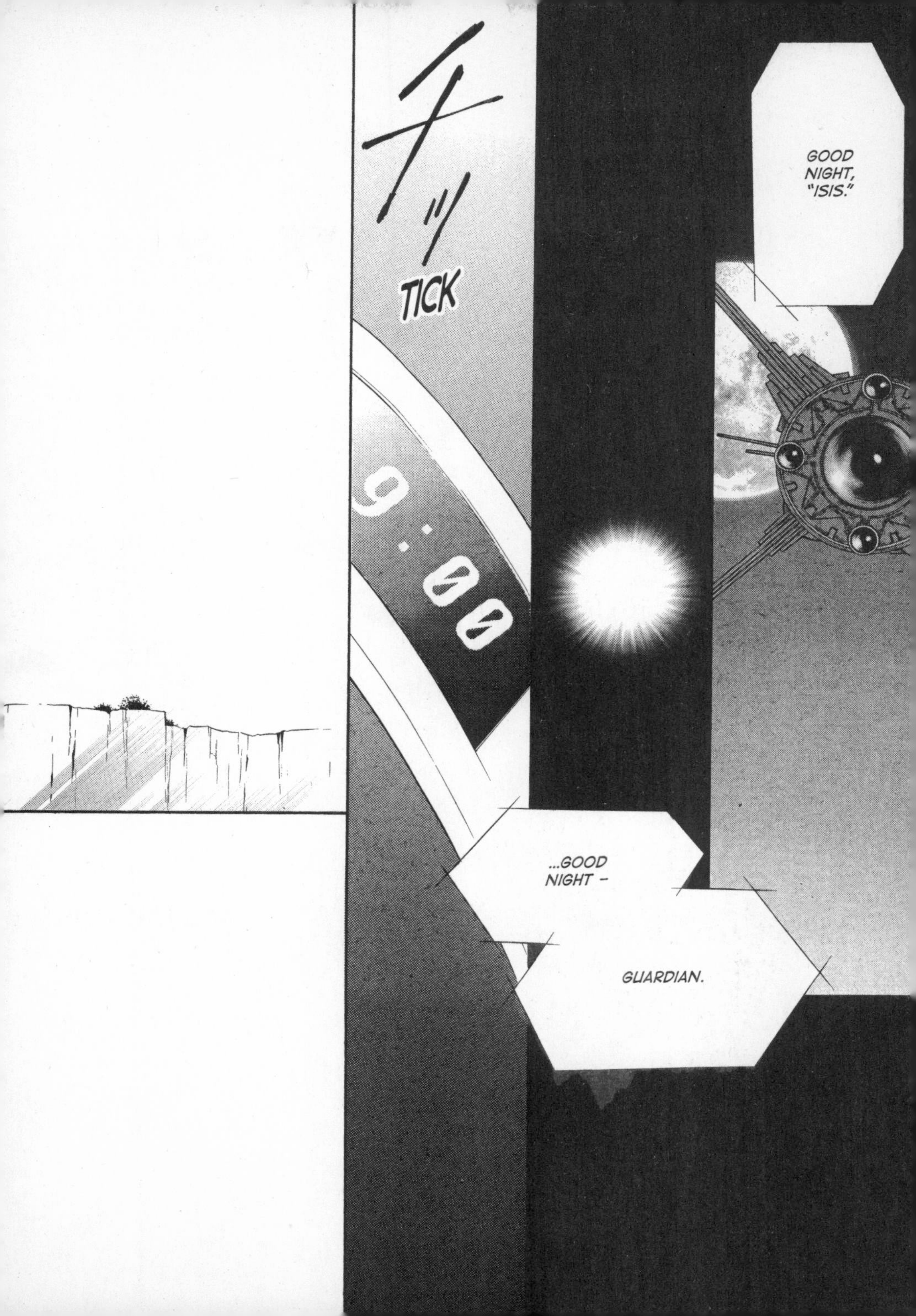
GOOD NIGHT, "ISIS."
...GOOD NIGHT -
GUARDIAN.
チッ
TICK
9:00

...THIS IS THE BEST DAY OF MY LIFE...!
PRESIDENT LESSINOS WINS BY A LANDSLIDE!
CHALLENGER BERNARDINO HAS BEEN DEFEATED !!
SNAP
... HMPH.
SO, HE LOST THIS TIME AROUND.
TOUGH LUCK, BERNARDINO.
OUCH...
I SWEAR...
IT WAS TERRIBLE. WE WERE SURROUNDED ON THE WAY HOME!
WHAT ABOUT YOU?
WE MANAGED SOME-HOW.
WHERE'S NOZOMI ?
HE'S OUTSIDE.

THAT'S SOME KID –
HE SNATCHED HIS LOVER BACK FROM THE ARMS OF DEATH.
EVEN "ISIS" PALES IN COMPARISON, EH?
NOW YOU CAN BE IN EACH OTHERS' ARMS ALL YOU WANT.

NO ONE...
IS SPYING ON YOU ANYMORE.
Steal Moon #8/ END

AFTERWORD

YEAH! WE MADE IT TO THE END!
THANK YOU VERY MUCH FOR READING THIS FAR.
I'M RELIEVED THAT I WAS ABLE TO FINISH THE STORY PROPERLY.

IN THE PREVIOUS VOLUME, IF YOU RECALL, I WAS FAINTING FROM HUNGER. MY DOCTOR EVENTUALLY ALLOWED ME TO ONCE AGAIN EAT CARBOHYDRATES, AND NOW I'M BACK TO MY BAD OLD EATING HABITS.
I WANT TO GO OUT AND PLAY -
HOWEVER, THE PUFFINESS IN MY LIMBS WENT AWAY AND HASN'T COME BACK, SO EVEN THOUGH MY LIFESTYLE IS STILL SEDENTARY, IT'S MORE COMFORTABLE.

"STEAL MOON" IS FINISHED NOW, BUT...
...BY THE TIME THIS VOLUME COMES OUT, I WILL BE DRAWING "BLUE SHEEP REVERIE 2," STARRING KAI AND LAHTI, FOR "KAREN" COMICS.
I HOPE YOU'LL CHECK THAT TITLE OUT AS WELL. WELL, THEN! I HOPE TO SEE YOU ALL SOON!! THIS HAS BEEN TATENO.
AFTERWORD / END

DIGITAL MANGA IS PROUD TO PRESENT
ITS NEWEST MANGA LINE:
Doki Doki
SHOWCASING THE BEST AND BRIGHTEST OF
ROMANCE, DRAMA AND COMEDY FROM DMP
AND SHINSHOKAN!
MIKIYO TSUDA
FULL-SIZED ARTIST PAGE PRINTS
DRAWN AND SIGNED BY MIKIYO TSUDA!
BUY DOKI DOKI NOW!
AND GET A FREE SPECIAL
LIMITED PROMO ITEM* UPON
ONE-TIME ONLINE REGISTRATION!
LOG ON NOW AT:
WWW.DOKIDOKIBOOKS.COM
PROMO ITEM IS FREE, BUT SUBJECT TO SHIPPING AND HANDLING FEES.
ROMO ITEMS ARE LIMITED TO A FIRST COME, FIRST SERVE BASIS, AND
RE LIMITED TO ONE PROMO ITEM PER BOOK PURCHASE.
NCESS PRINCESS PLUS © MIKIYO TSUDA/SHINSHOKAN 2007. Originally published in Japan in 2007 by SHINSHOKAN CO., LTD.
IN TRAIN VOL. 1 © EIKI EIKI/SHINSHOKAN 2002. Originally published in Japan in 2002 by SHINSHOKAN CO., LTD.
Doki Doki FROM DMP 新書館 SHINSHOKAN

NOW YOU CAN READ YOUR FAVORITE
DMP BOOKS ONLINE AT
emanga
eマンガ.com
LET'S DRAW MANGA
ORIGINAL CONTENT
OUT OF PRINT TITLES
CHECK FREQUENTLY FOR SPECIAL PROMOTIONS!!
LOTS OF YAOI MANGA!
EXCLUSIVE ONLINE CONTENT
CHECK US OUT AT
EMANGA.COM
RED © Sanae Rokuya. All rights reserved. Original Japanese edition published in 2006 by Taiyoh Tosho Publishing Co., Ltd.
NEW BEGINNINGS - HARETE BOKUTACHIWA © KOTETSUKO YAMAMOTO. All rights reserved. Original Japanese edition published in 200
by Taiyoh Tosho Publishing Co., Ltd. Cho Ni Naru Hi / The Day I Become a Butterfly © Sumomo Yumeka 2005. Originally published in Japa
in 2003 by Taiyoh Tosho Co., Ltd. LOST BOYS © Kaname Itsuki 2004. Originally published in Japan in 2004 by Taiyoh Tosho Co., Ltd
DOUSAIBOU SEIBUTSU / SAME CELL ORGANISM © Sumomo 2001. Originally published in Japan in 2001 by Taiyoh Tosho Co., Ltd.
Let's Draw Manga - Drawing Yaoi © 2007 by DIGITAL MANGA, Inc. All rights reserved.

MW00791870
This is the back of the book!
Please start the book from the other side...
Native manga readers read manga from right to left to keep the manga true to its original vision. To enjoy, turn the book over and start from the other side and read right to left, top to bottom.
Follow the diagram to see how it's done!
3
1
2
2
1
3
6
5
5
4
8
6
7
4
NATIVE MANGA
READ RIGHT TO LEFT
If you see the logo above, you'll know that this book is published in its original native format.
Yaoi
ヤオイ
Manga